JUNIE'S STORY

A Special Wish From a Little Dog Who Lost Her Forever Home

Narrated by Junie

Paula Bourassa

Junie's Story

ISBN: 978-0-9993197-8-9

Dedicated to Sara

Special Thank You to Auntie M and Uncle J

CONTENTS

Pound to Pet Store

My life began in a big place with lots of cages called a puppy mill, but soon after providing them with puppies, I was thrown out and had to leave my furry babies behind. I was only a baby myself at nine months old and didn't know what I would do.

Someone saw me scavenging in the street and called animal control. An agency for homeless animals took me to another room full of cages. I had to stay behind bars, was all alone, and did not understand why.

One day, a lady and her daughter came to visit so I felt extremely excited and perked up. The girl had been promised a dog for getting good grades in school, however, after being with them just a short week, she decided I was too much trouble and didn't want to take care of me anymore. Back to the shelter I went to behind bars with a hurting heart and alone.

I was getting food there, but no pets or cuddles. Pretty soon a group of angel people came and rescued all of us in cages. We were taken to a temporary home where they prepared us for adoption. Our first chance would be at the locale pet store.

I was in an outstanding position being the first one in the upper row. We'd been lined up in a certain way so that customers could see each one of us clearly, but I was nervous and could not stop shaking. Before long, a man and two women walked over to stand in front of my crate. He was talking about finding a companion for his wife who spent most days alone while he was away long hours at work.

They stood there looking at me. My heart was pounding loudly when he opened the door and even though I was trembling, managed to crawl right up unto his shoulder. He looked so tall and sturdy I clutched him and never wanted to let go.
The agency people said that I was a Jack

Russel terrier mix named Bella and that I was stressed from losing my past two homes in such a brief time. The man and his wife liked that I was so willing to be part of their family and said they would like me to go home with them.

They received my health and history information and agreed to have background checks done of themselves. The special people wanted to make sure I would not be in a home where someone would intentionally try to hurt me or just not take care of me at all! They were Pet Angels on Earth.

During the time the angle people were making sure I would be in good hands, the man and ladies walked around all the cages set up that day and said prayers each animal would find the most perfect owner. That made me feel good they cared about everyone there.

They even found another little dog who was my size and looked like me, but when they put me in a separate room to meet him, I started growling and was not very friendly, so my new parents agreed that I should be an only child. I did not mean to sound angry I was just nervous and unsure of the situation.

It all happened so quickly before I knew what was going on, I was getting into a car with my new owners. They thought I was a gift of joy and love and since it was the first month of summer, they decided to call me "Junie." I was in the backseat admiring my new parents and they were super happy to have me because they noticed my enthusiasm and gave me the middle name of Joy. I was their new family member, Junie Joy.

Tip 1

Please give a home to an animal
who already needs one if you can

Junie Finds Her Forever Home

The couple of the house considered themselves to be forever partners, and so they reassured me that I'd found my forever place too and didn't need to worry about getting returned this time. My mommy wanted me to understand I was safe and would never need to search for someone to take care of me again.

Mommy and I spent many hours together because she worked from the computer. I was her new best friend and got hugs and kisses. I did not have a very good appetite, so she played a fun eating game with me.

She would kneel by my dish and say in a low growl voice, "I'm going to eat this food!" repeating it over and over until I felt territorial about my kibble and let out little yelps that meant, "No, I am going to eat it and gobble it up quickly." Then, I would hunker down over the food dish ravishing every morsel till all gone. Phew, mommy would feel relieved that I ate.

I was timid and mommy was smart enough to know I needed some help in the food department. Being in the puppy mill had left me anxious about feeding time because I always worried if it was ok to eat my food or if I should just let the other dogs take it from me.

My Auntie P was on hand to witness some of our activities. She would enjoy late afternoons when I would listen for the sound of daddy's car pulling into the driveway and excitedly greet him at the door. Daddy would walk in the house and wait for me to jump up on the high part of the sofa where I'd perch until he scooped me up, turn me on my back, and plant a big fat smooch on my belly.

Tip 2 🐾

Always make sure
your pet has food
and water

Then, he would set me down and I would race after him on his way toward the bedroom where he'd lay down for some TV time with mommy. First though, he would grab a few leftover snacks from his lunch bag to take with him and I'd try to look as cute as possible to show him they were of interest to me.

Daddy would fall asleep early after a hard day at work and mommy would stay up late. I had the best of both worlds and would spend some time sleeping by daddy's legs, and then when it got to hot, would run out and lay on the sofa near mommy's computer table.

Mommy was always at home and seldom went anywhere, so it was like having a great safety net over me. We were a close-knit family, and I was the esteemed child. If mom and dad went for a drive, I got to join them so I wouldn't have to stay home alone. I was a happy girl because I had found my forever home!

Tip 3

Please treat your pets like family members

Oh No!

One night at bedtime, mommy felt sick, so daddy offered her some stomach medicine. She didn't want to go to the hospital but felt certain that if she'd just lay back down on her side, the symptoms would improve.

They laid down together, but an hour later when Dad woke up, Mommy did not. She never woke up again. When the paramedics came, I licked her face wanting to help but they thought I was in their way and quickly locked me away in another room.

I was so sad to see Mommy like that. She was my whole life, my rock. They raced off to the hospital and I was alone in that room it seemed for a long time. Many hours later, daddy came home alone. I jumped up by his side to make him feel better, but we were both too sad. The rest of the day I watched the front door for mommy to come, but she never did. I watched the door for many days, but only my two aunties came in and out.

Mom's daughter, Auntie D, and her best friend, Auntie P, were both there trying to help me and daddy. I lost my appetite, so they tried all sorts of tricks to get me to eat. They put soup broth on my kibble, and even a spoonful of pumpkin, but nothing sounded good because Mommy wasn't there to eat with me.

Everyone worried, so Auntie D went out and found a special refrigerated food with carrots and cranberries in it. It smelled so good I ate it up, but only if someone sat with me by my dish so I wasn't alone. I waited to be hand fed because it was the only way I could get the food down.

Auntie P was part of our family, so she knew some of my habits. When I'd put my paws upon her legs and looked deep into her eyes, she knew that was signal for me needing potty outside. In the morning, I would stand by the back sliding patio door, and she recognized that was my way of saying I wanted to go into the backyard to sun.

Thank goodness my aunties were there, and daddy also got some help for errands and extra support. We were all deeply upset, especially daddy. Mommy had been his entire world and reason for getting up every morning.

One day everyone left the house for several hours. I was so happy when they got back, I ran round and round the house in circles jumping up on the back of their knees to let them know how excited I was they returned. I had been very worried no one would come back. If mommy could leave me, anyone could leave me.

Daddy spent most of his time in bed too saddened to do anything else. My aunties would stay up late and talk, so I still had two places to run back and forth for my evening routine, Daddy's bed, and then back out to the front room with aunties.

Tip 4

Never abandon your pet and make sure they have someone to take care of them, especially if you leave home or can't take them with you

Now No Daddy!

I woke up one morning only six days after mommy disappeared to find daddy missing. We had gone to bed the night before and sometime during the dark hours I jumped down to go out and make potty on my papers.

Usually, he would tell me it was ok to jump back up on the bed but this time when I came back, no word from daddy, so I jumped into my little bed alongside his instead. He was not getting up for work, so I stayed quiet.

My aunties had gone outside while special persons came in to see if they could help daddy get out of bed. He didn't seem to notice I was there or anyone else. Pretty soon, they put daddy on a long flat bed and took him outside into a van.

One of the helpers put a rope around me and took me out to where my aunties were waiting on the curb. We were incredibly happy to see each other. We were all shook up. First mommy gone and now daddy, all in the same week.

I jumped into Auntie P's arms and got to stay cuddled there until I calmed down. The big van and other cars drove away and as I sat and watched the front door, daddy never came back home either. Each day, I listened for the sound of his car but only heard auntie's car. One day auntie went to pick me up and she heard me let out a pitiful noise that she said sounded like a cry of grief.

Tip 5

Remember animals have feelings just like you!

Daddy had been so upset he missed a package in the mail from mommy for Father's Day. It was a T-shirt for him that said "The Dogfather" on the front, and on the back was a picture of me and daddy sitting side by side. He would have been so proud that mommy honored him this way, but he never received his gift. Mom and Dad were both gone, and my forever home completely crumbled.

My aunties had many discussions about what would happen to me. Auntie P offered to take me because daddy said if anything ever happened to him, I should go with her. Mommy had a sister, Auntie L, who loved me too, but she had two other doggies and that would make me number three.

Mom and dad always said I was meant to be the only one. Mom's other daughter, Auntie J, lived close by and offered to take me, but she had many people living in her house and aunties thought all the extra noises might scare me.

So, it was Auntie P who took me on a flight back to her apartment in a faraway city. It was very scary because of big booms and shakes in the dark, and all I could see was other people with masks on their faces. Auntie worried about me because my heart never stopped thumping and I was panting the whole time with yucky breath because I was so nervous.

We were lucky though, because the people sat next to us on the airplane were very friendly and didn't seem to mind, which my auntie told them after we landed how grateful she was for their kindness.

My New Home

Auntie P's sister, my new Auntie M, and her husband Uncle J, picked us up at the airport. This was a good thing because auntie was having trouble managing me, a backpack, and two suitcases. It was a long ride but after three hours, I arrived at my new home. It was all different, the weather, the rooms, and the smells.

I had been indoors most of the time and wasn't used to going outside except for a quick front or back lawn visit. I had been paper trained because I didn't like to get my feet wet, so for bad weather, mommy had taught me how to go on papers inside the house.

Auntie P spent lots of time in nature, so in my new location I was excited to make potty outdoors. One day it was misting rain and she took me out for a walk. I was so worried I might get left behind, I hadn't even noticed it was raining and ended up soaking wet. Auntie saw my surprise when we got home and quickly towel dried me to get some of the water off. Wow, I did it. I got wet.

Doggies love to go outside for fresh air and to smell stuff. They cannot ask you to put a jacket on them or take one off, so please make sure they are never too warm or cold

Tip 6

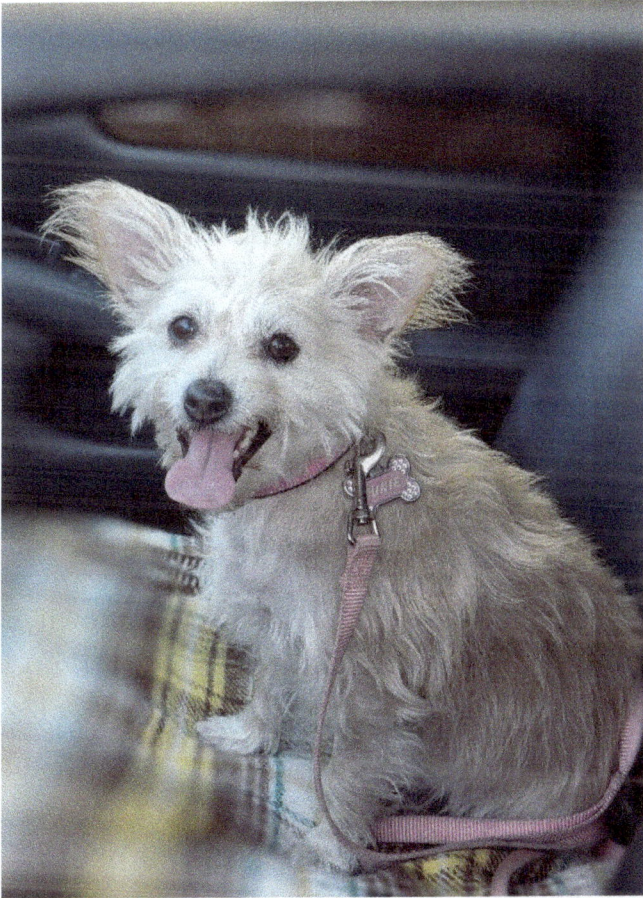

There were lots of new sights and sounds. It was difficult for me to concentrate on my business with the grinds, bangs, and roars of car noises. Auntie remembered something mommy would say if I was taking too long to make potty, she would say "Junie, Focus!" If I was smelling around too much auntie would say the same thing, "Junie, Focus!"

By far though, the biggest shake-up was the sound of a big flock of geese overhead! They were in some kind family group meeting in the sky and flew so loudly over us, I stood shaking not sure if they wanted something from me. I never saw a goose before!

It gave me bad dreams for a couple of days with whimpers in my sleep, but I got over it. I was grateful for a roof over my head and appreciated my auntie, but still looked for mommy and daddy everyplace. I had an especially tough time if Auntie P went to take the trash out. Those few minutes seemed like an awful long time.

One day on a visit to my new grama's house, I jumped up to sit on the chair with her while

Auntie P went to visit her brother down the street. I was over the moon an hour later when she came back, but Grama C reported that when she let me outside to see if I needed potty, I'd sat in the middle of the driveway instead, staring toward where the car had been parked. Grama felt sad about this, but I couldn't help wondering where Auntie P and the car had gone. I worried about people not coming back.

I enjoyed going for walks because it took my mind off missing mommy and daddy. One day we were walking down the side of a street when we saw a cat in the middle of the road swishing his tail back and forth without a care in the world. I had never seen an animal like that and started to tremble.

Auntie picked me up as she bent over to speak to him explaining it wasn't a good idea to be sitting like a statute in the middle of a road. She said he looked young and didn't realize he could get hurt if a car came zooming by, and in a firm voice tried to make him understand that.

I was in auntie's arms the whole time, but she set me back down when it was safe again further down the way. What a surprise I had when Mr. Cat came running from behind and jumped on my back thinking I might want to play if he got some games started. I froze in terror until auntie picked me up again, but when I felt her smile, I calmed down and realized everything must be ok.

Tip 7

Never hurt an animal and help your pets to get along with other animals even though they have differences

Hands of Love

I wasn't sure how long my new home would last but came to trust that I was loved forever, even if my first few homes didn't work out. My auntie loved me, and my old and new relatives all loved me, so I was lucky. I still had love. Love was my home.

A good example was at my new grandma's house was when she let me jump up on her sofa and lay my head on the pillow. I felt like a princess and one of her special granddaughters to receive such royal treatment. I was very fond of people who like to sit down and stay there a long time! I overheard my aunties saying I was a real lapdog, but also wanted to say that I am also a love-dog, thanks to all the people here, there, and everywhere who've offered me love and support.

Give your pet a comfortable place to rest

Tip 8

Auntie P shared that even though nothing lasts forever, she promised me she'd make sure I was always in the hand of love, so my dream is for every doggie, for every pet, to have a home or place on Earth where they can feel hands of love too!

And if you cannot find a hand, a foot will do!

A special tribute to the foot of a man, Jose Tavera, who exemplified kindness in his every interaction with all of God's living things.

www.ingramcontent.com/pod-product-compliance
Lightning Source LLC
Chambersburg PA
CBHW060042040426
42331CB00032B/2244